IT'S NOT PMS, IT'S YOU!

IT'S NOT PMS,

IT'S YOU!

A Totally Non-Hormonal Analysis of Male Behavior

DEB AMLEN

STERLING INNOVATION

An imprint of Sterling Publishing Co., Inc.

New York / London
www.sterlingpublishing.com

Library of Congress Cataloging-in-Publication Data

Amlen, Deb.

It's not PMS, it's you! : a totally non-hormonal analysis of male behavior
/ Deb Amlen.

p. cm.

ISBN 978-1-4027-7031-9

1. Men--Humor. 2. Man-woman relationships--Humor. 3. Dating
(Social customs)--Humor. I. Title.

PN6231.M45A54 2010

818'.5402--dc22

2009036514

10 9 8 7 6 5 4 3 2 1

Published by Sterling Publishing Co., Inc.
387 Park Avenue South, New York, NY 10016
© 2010 by Sterling Publishing Co., Inc.
Distributed in Canada by Sterling Publishing
c/o Canadian Manda Group, 165 Dufferin Street
Toronto, Ontario, Canada M6K 3H6
Distributed in the United Kingdom by GMC Distribution Services
Castle Place, 166 High Street, Lewes, East Sussex, England BN7 1XU
Distributed in Australia by Capricorn Link (Australia) Pty. Ltd.
P.O. Box 704, Windsor, NSW 2756, Australia

Printed in China
All rights reserved

Design by Alicia Freile, Tango Media

Sterling ISBN 978-1-4027-7031-9

For information about custom editions, special sales, premium and
corporate purchases, please contact Sterling Special Sales
Department at 800-805-5489 or specialsales@sterlingpublishing.com.

For my family
and
for my dear friend Nancy Prater,
who would have loved this

TABLE OF CONTENTS

WHAT GIVES HER THE RIGHT? Y'KNOW?!

If you happen to be a person of the male variety, you may have picked up this book thinking that it looked like an excellent way to better understand the female psyche (a closely guarded military secret, so good luck with that). You may have even wondered what kind of high-level, scientific expertise was needed to meld the years of research and hours of complex computer analysis necessary to answer such inscrutable questions as: "Is eating straight out of the fridge really such a bad thing?"; "How are pork rinds *not* an appetizer suitable for company?"; or even "Doesn't *everyone* find the phrase 'Nyuck nyuck nyuck' absolutely, rip-snorting hilarious?"

At least a Nobel Prize winner, you bet. And you'd be wrong, because this is not that kind of book. If you are trying to find out why the woman in your life spends at least one week each month as an unreasonable psycho who swigs Bosco straight from the bottle, you will not find it here. This is about you, guys. And we're going to hit the ground running, so hold on to your hats. If you're wearing one, that is.

Because for every woman who ever pulled her hair out trying to explain—for the 46th time—the importance of putting the toilet seat *down*, for Christ's sake, or that burping the national anthem after every meal is *not* a constitutional right, there have been entire herds of men who, nodding sagely in unison, have made the mistake of saying, "Must be that time of the month."

For every woman who has rolled her eyes through yet another evening of Grand Theft Auto when she could have been out dancing on tables in restaurants with sexy Latin waiters, there have been men popping up like weeds snickering, "Someone's on the rag."

Come to think of it, this is a book for all of us, an attempt to both educate and heal, to deeply bury the hatchet (not that it would occur to us). Inside these pages is an attempt to analyze and forgive the behavior of the half of the human population that still believes that a good fart joke will ease those awkward silences on a first date.

Now pass me that bottle of Bosco and let's get started.

CHAPTER 1

THE HISTORY OF BEING "ON THE RAG"

Don't you just hate it when you've had an absolute bear of a day upholstering furniture, making uniforms for the entire Continental Army, plowing the north forty and trying not to die of typhus, when some guy and his stupid friends drop by asking you to create a flag out of basically nothing while they're out "founding the country," and then they keep *changing* the number of stars they want on it, and *changing* the number of stripes they want on it until you're convinced that it must be a prank and you just want to run them all through with your bodkin?

Of course you do. Because even before the dawn of ironclad prenuptial agreements, the men and women of past civilizations had many of the same communication problems we face today. Oh sure, we could continue to swallow the guano our history books feed us about our country being made what it is today by the hard work and sacrifice of our four fathers—John, Paul, George, and Ringo[1]—but don't think for a second that behind every brave, tricornered-hat-wearing, musket-toting patriot there wasn't an equally brave patriot-ess with 16 children, a homestead to run, no civil rights and an enormous bone to pick.

In fact, it goes back much, much further than that. Scientists have uncovered indisputable evidence[2] that from the time we clomped out of the primordial soup, Bosco in hand, millions of years ago (or 1492, if you're counting by Intelligent Design Method, or IDM), couples have been arguing about many of the same things you and your significant other argue about today.

[1] *Editor's Note:* Don't believe anything she says. I happen to know she failed Western Civilization in school. Twice.
[2] *Editor's Note:* What scientists? What evidence? Did she fact-check *any* of this?!
Author's Note: No.

Perhaps the worst era for relationships was during the lifetime of *Homo Neanderthalensis*, also known in scientific circles as the Flintstone Period (1571–1632 IDM). Artifacts from this period have revealed startling evidence that fire was actually first cultivated and tamed by a woman, but take a gander at the pictures in any history book and what do you see? A bunch of cavemen gathered around the fire pit, patting each other on their hairy backs, and generally taking credit for a woman's work.

This is not to say, however, that ancient man was not responsible for some marvelous inventions of his own, usually inspired by fermented beverages and his group of cave buddies. As time went on and their knowledge of fire-taming grew, the male members of the tribe discovered that if one of them judiciously selected a dry stick, touched it carefully to the fire until it caught a spark, and held it ever so carefully behind himself, he could, using only the power of his digestive system, shoot that baby a good ten feet or so, thus inventing the first gas-powered blowtorch.

Even creative outlets for Neanderthal man led to misunderstandings. These primitive men, inspired by the beauty around them and the mysteries of life,  and showing an almost poignant desire to leave a record for those who would come later, developed important rituals around painting large, intricate murals depicting their short, brutal lives. These pictorial stories ritualistically revealed the drama of the hunt, the triumph of providing food for the clan, or the wonders of the circle of life, and ritualistically stretched the entire length of the cave wall, often right over the heirloom armoire that the primitive woman had inherited from her grandmother ("Dammit, Oog, I just cleaned that!").

As primitive woman ritualistically scoured the walls and furniture, ranting about how she was *not* a magician and how bison blood and berry juice stains don't just come out of furniture by themselves, the cavemen gathered in groups, scratching their heads and wondering what in Ur's name they had done wrong. Of course, rags had not been invented yet, so all primitive man could come up with as a witty retort was, "Boy, looks like *someone* is squatting on a pelt in the Cave of Untouchable Women."

In fact, archaeologists have recently uncovered evidence of such an event, consisting primarily of male skeletal remains with what seems to be a primitive paintbrush jammed in his esophagus. Scientists now conclude that this ancient ritual was ended prematurely by a primitive woman who had heard the pelt line one too many times, and is on record as the first-ever breakup.

Of course, things had improved a bit by the time the Middle Ages rolled around (1955–1978 IDM). For one thing, rags had finally been invented, although at this point they were still strictly the domain of the lower classes, who used them primarily to keep from freezing to death. The upper classes and nobility of the day, lacking this important resource, struggled to give words to the communication problems that continued to plague them.

William Shakespeare ("lulling high school students to sleep since 1585") wrote about this in *Hamlet,* one of the classic, feel-good relationship stories of the day. Hamlet, of course, was the prince of Denmark, a country that apparently receives so little sunlight that everyone in the play walks around all depressed and weepy, and pretty much everyone in the play eventually winds up dead. Experts who can actually understand what the hell Shakespeare was talking about point to this play as one of the epic breakup stories of all time.

The gist of the story, as far as anyone can tell, is that while his girlfriend, Ophelia, is more than happy to work on their relationship and hopes it will lead to marriage, Hamlet is being all pissy and preoccupied because his father's ghost is pressuring him to avenge his death and put asunder the incestuous marriage 'twixt his widow and his brother. So far, something we can all relate to, right?

Meanwhile, things progress pretty much the way you'd expect in a Shakespearean drama, with lots of court intrigue and language no one understands, until Ophelia is taken aside by her father and brother and told, in florid and practically unintelligible words, "Forsooth, he's just not that into you."

Not that Ophelia is beginning to suspect that something is up. After all, the classic signs are there: He avoids her to spend a lot of time with his guy friends. He's not returning her calls. Worst of all, he seems to prefer spending all of his time lately pondering the meaning of life, and, honestly, how many times can she listen to him drone on and on about such a depressing topic? It's not like he's in any danger of killing himself, right?

And then there's the whole thing with her dad. In what is possibly the most spectacular example of Problem In-Law Management ever, Hamlet kills her father by running him through with his sword and defensively claiming that he was just trying to rid his mother's wardrobe of vermin. ("My bad. What was he doing in the closet anyway?") You just don't get over that so quickly.

So our girl Ophelia decides to take things into her own hands and tries to give Hamlet the ol' heave-ho. This is where things get really nasty. Predictably, Hamlet does not take the news well, and, revealing the classic abandonment issues that would not be professionally diagnosed for at least another 400 years, proceeds to call her every demeaning Elizabethan name in the book.

Now remember, Hamlet and Ophelia were members of the Danish nobility, so the one thing he *couldn't* do was accuse her of being on the rag, mostly due to sensitive copyright issues with the lower class. Instead, upper class women who found themselves in this sort of trouble were typically accused of being witches, and, in keeping with the advanced legal and medical wisdom of the day, thrown into the nearest body of water. If you floated, it was bad news: you were now officially clean enough to be executed. If you sank, however, all was forgiven: you were dead, but clearly not bewitched.

Anyway, all of this hoo-ha with Hamlet grates on poor Ophelia until she becomes an absolute, raving wack-job, and in a gripping scene where we're pretty sure she calls him a couple of choice names herself, she bids a poignant farewell to the court of Elsinore and hurls her *own* damn self into the nearest body of water, where of course she sinks like a rock. This leads Hamlet to deliver the now-famous and highly dramatic soliloquy, "She Had It Coming," and ends what is clearly one of the most toxic relationships in literary history.

This brings us to the Victorian Era (January 6, 2010 IDM), named for the Queen of England at the time and apparently created solely for Dame Judi Dench, who is the only person allowed to play her in the movies.[3]

The social mores of this period forbade the kind of public bickering of the Middle Ages and made the Moral Majority look like residents of the Playboy Mansion. Name-calling and profanity were out. Vulgarity of all kinds was replaced by the use of euphemisms, a far more civilized tradition of using refined words so as not to offend.

Naturally this led to all sorts of frustration, because while our brains are perfectly happy to recall any given obscenity or insult at a moment's notice, it takes considerably more time for them to come up with a less offensive substitute.

[3] Seriously. It's in her contract. (*Editor's Note:* No, it's not. Stop that!)

Victorian Man 1: What did you just say to me?!

Victorian Man 2: I said, Your wife is . . . not ugly, what's that word that means ugly but is not as strong?

Victorian Man 1: Unattractive?

Victorian Man 2: Oh yes. I'm not saying your wife is unattractive but . . . No wait. Your wife is so plain that . . . No, that's no good either.

Victorian Man 1: *(looking at watch)* Is this going to take long?

Victorian Man 2: Got it! Your wife's general countenance is so plain that it makes children feel uncertain. Hey, where'd he go?

Most historians now agree that this tradition pretty much sucked all of the fun out of a good argument. History also tells us that despite the social restrictions of the time, Victoria and her consort, Prince Albert, engaged in some epic battles behind the walls of the castle.

After a night of "carousing"—a Victorian euphemism for chugging beer from a lady's shoe[4]—Albert was not above "fluffing the covers," another charming Victorian euphemism for making sure nooky was out for the night, and a habit that drove Victoria absolutely batty.

Taking a page from Sir George Bernard Shaw's magnum opus, *Telephone Pranks for All Ages*, she finally put a stop to it by locking him in "the can," as it was known in Victorian parlance, and not releasing him until he could get one of his friends to call and beg her to let him out.

This was harder than it sounds, because Victoria could be a real stickler for protocol:

Victoria: Hello?

Albert's Friend: I say, Your Majesty, is Albert there?

Victoria: That's not how you say it.

Albert's Friend: Oh dear. He's locked in the loo, sorry, "the can" again, isn't he?

Victoria: That's not it either.

Albert's Friend: Your Majesty, this is the third time this week.

[4] A tradition involving the consumption of enough alcohol in order to avoid thinking about the fact that Odor Eaters had not yet been invented.

Victoria: Well, we are not amused.

Albert's Friend: We all get that, Your Highness, but . . . oh all right! *(reading from crib note)* Have you got Prince Albert in a can?

Victoria: *(snickering)* Yes.

Albert's Friend: Well then, you'd better let him out.

Victoria: Da ha ha ha ha ha ha ha ha ha!

While this didn't do much for the evolution of relationships, it did pave the way for running refrigerator jokes everywhere (rim shot).

And speaking of refrigerators, we next lurch gracefully into the industry- and technology-driven 20th and 21st centuries (although these technically don't yet exist in IDM). In an age as modern as this, rags are now available to anyone who wants them, and men and women have finally evolved to the point where misunderstandings are laughed off, all relationships are smooth sailing, and everyone just kind of gets along. Right?

Let's do a quick recap and see whether that theory holds true:

- We've progressed past the point where a man would even think about taking credit for a woman's work, haven't we?
- Your average guy is mature enough to tell a woman straight out if he's not into her, and would *never* think of committing any passive-aggressive acts to indicate as much, right?
- This same average guy is now so evolved that he no longer finds anything even remotely funny about fart jokes, right?

Right???
Uh oh.

CHAPTER 2

HOW THEY GET THIS WAY

OK, time for a quick survey.

Hands up, those of you who believe that the quirky male behavior we've all come to know and love—we keep going back for more, don't we?—is a sudden and alarming change, kind of like Dr. Jekyll and Mr. Hyde, that takes place on a young man's 21st birthday. Now hands up, those of you who, after being in one or two doozy relationships, have come to believe that this same behavior could *only* be the result of careful and deliberate training dating from childhood, involving cherished-yet-clueless traditions passed down from father to son eventually leading to clandestine meetings and oaths of brotherhood taken under the full moon.

That's what I thought. Hands down. We'll get back to that in a moment.

When I had my first baby, a big topic of discussion amongst the young mothers in my neighborhood was the debate over whether giving children "gender neutral" toys would encourage the girls to think past traditional female roles and make boys more sensitive and nurturing. At the time, it seemed like a reasonable idea: a girl who plays with cars and trucks might develop an interest in a nontraditional career, like automotive engineering; a boy who plays with dolls may develop the nurturing skills he needs to be a good father someday, or, if he went in a different direction, an interest in hairdressing or fashion design.

To women like myself who grew up with fewer choices, this seemed to be the way to raise the perfect child. This was the 1990s, mind you, when perfection seemed to be the ultimate goal. Most of us had wandered over to motherhood from the business world, where the constant babble about standards of excellence and perfection had been taken to an almost aerobic level. ("Get those sales goals UP, ladies! And HIGHER, two, three, four . . . And BREATHE! . . . ") So it made perfect sense to us that if we could raise perfect children in a perfect and gender neutral way, we could all sit back and enjoy our perfect lives until we were on our perfect deathbeds and we would eventually realize that we'd all forgotten to have any fun.

Boy, what a bunch of noobs we were. Not only *didn't* it matter what toys the kids were given to play with—most of them thought it was more fun to put the plastic packaging over their heads, anyway, cute and heart-attack-inducing little tykes that they were—but half the time their true natures led them to play with the toys in ways that showed we'd done nothing but confuse them. I'm a veteran of a *lot* of playdates, and have personally witnessed little girls wrapping dump trucks in blankets and singing to them, not to mention boys who, in a pinch, think that the "Havin'-It-All Chief Executive Officer Barbie" that Mommy bought them makes a swell baseball bat. Bonus points if her head comes flying off when you hit a home run.

Don't get me wrong. I'm *not* saying we shouldn't expand our children's horizons or teach them to think outside the gender box. But if you go to great lengths to buy a non-traditional and educational toy and the box is the only thing your child is interested in, maybe the kid should be allowed to make the choice from now on, is all I'm saying.

This became more apparent to me when I had my second child five years later. This one was a boy, and I was still determined to raise him with gender neutral toys, although I will admit that by then the perfection thing was getting a bit exhausting. As a young child, he had inherited a small tribe of Pokémon figurines from his sister and needed a place for them to live. What a perfect opportunity, thought I, to teach him all about communal living and household responsibilities. Somewhere in the ether, I swore I could hear the veteran mothers who had come before me laughing until they lactated all over their spit-up-stained sweatshirts. Undeterred, out I went in search of a small dollhouse for my son.

He was absolutely delighted. It had plenty of rooms for the Pokémon to wander through, yet it was small enough to carry around. He held it in his small hands, admiring it from all angles. He spent quite some time filling the rooms with his figurines, patiently tolerating my background chatter about how Pokémon, like everyone else, have to be able to live together and share their things. When it was filled to his satisfaction, he gently placed it on an ottoman in the center of the room and backed away, admiring his work. Isn't that amazing, I thought, he's taking in this wonderful family living scene. Before I could stop him, he crouched down in perfect linebacker form, lowered his head, and ran full tilt at it, headbutting the poor Pokémon and their new home into oblivion. My jaw dropped.

"Why would you do that?!" I gasped, horrified by the Pokécarnage around me.

"They moved in just before the Death Star hit," he replied matter-of-factly.

This was a watershed moment in my life as a woman, a wife, and a mother. Could the quirks I attributed to my husband and some of the adult males around me be, in fact, something that is already in a boy's DNA, something that is automatically transmitted through bloodlines dating back to prerecorded history? Or could it be—*cue ominous music*—that the brotherhood just got to them first?

Turns out it's probably a little of both. We all know that this type of behavior goes way back, but what do we do when the training takes place in the home and is also a traditional part of their education?

Somewhere around middle school, kids in our country are shepherded, boys and girls separately, into classrooms to be alternately confused and embarrassed by courageous teaching professionals who are entrusted with the job of explaining the facts of life to them. Opinions about sex education in school vary widely in this country, and while I'm *not* saying that it should not be taught, I will go on record as suggesting that perhaps the people we allow to educate our children in this way should receive some additional training before undertaking this endeavor. I'm referring specifically to the male gym teacher in a friend's community who told the boys in his charge "not to worry too much if the girls get all emotional and upset during their 'minstrel' cycle." Lord knows what the poor boys were envisioning at that point, but I'm thinking it gave more meaning to "monthly change" than they were bargaining for.

But the training is still the primary job of the father, as far as anyone can tell. Take my friends Lori and Ed,[5] for example. Anyone who knows Lori and Ed knows that they are a wonderful couple, happy in their marriage and fabulous parents. Ed works a lot, but participates in the raising of his child and is an all-around modern dad. In every way but one.

One day, when their son, Robby, was about two, Lori needed to go out for the day to visit her mother and left Ed in charge. Before she left, she diligently cooked two breakfasts, two lunches, and two dinners so they would both have something to eat. She did the laundry, folded it, and put it away so they would have clothes to wear. Lori carefully made a list of doctors' phone numbers and emergency contacts in case something went wrong, and even got out some toddler-

[5] Names have been changed to protect the innocent and the guilty, respectively.

safe toys so they could do some fun father and son bonding.

So they played with the toddler toys and ate the meals Lori had made. When they got bored with that, they played Superman and Super Boy, Robby's favorite pretend dress-up game involving capes and superpowers. By early evening, Superman, who was not really used to running after a toddler all day, was pretty exhausted. He had also forgotten to put Super Boy down for his nap, so they were both getting a mite cranky.

"If we can just make it through dinner," Superman told his son brightly, using the perky tone people use when talking to someone they think is of lesser intelligence, "I've got it made. Mommy will be home soon and I'll be off duty."

"Doody!" Super Boy cheerfully agreed, pointing to his diaper.

"*Off* duty," the Man of Steel repeated. "Daddy will be off duty."

"*DOO-dy!*" Super Boy warned, at the exact moment the smell wafted toward Superman's nose.

Those of you who have ever had a toddler in your possession will understand what I'm talking about when I say that this was the kind of epic poop that cannot be contained by any diaper on the consumer market. Scientists who have studied toddler food-intake-to-poop ratios have been known to quit their jobs and find other, less traumatizing lines of work when confronted with the kind of poop Robby produced that day.

A horrible idea began to form in Ed's mind. He still had about an hour to go until Lori got home. It was wrong of him, he knew, but if he could just put off the inevitable until she got back, he could pass the buck, so to speak, to his wife.

When Lori walked through the door that evening, this is the scene that lay before her:

- One grown man, asleep and snoring on the living room couch with a towel masquerading as a cape tied around his neck and a construction paper 'S' taped to his chest;
- One small child, naked except for a dirty diaper and cape/towel, *standing up* in front of the couch with his head on a pillow, also fast asleep;

- A pile of toddler clothing on the floor with a sign on it that said, "BURN ME."

Just for the hell of it, Lori decided to wake Ed and ask the questions any sane person stumbling upon a scene like this would ask: "Not for nothing, but what the heck happened here? Why didn't you just change his diaper?"

And Ed, in all seriousness, looked his wife straight in the eye and said, "We were thinking it might be kryptonite."

Here's my point: even though little Robby was only two and might not consciously remember this experience, you just *know* that one day he will have a child of his own, and he too will hook him onto a couch and make him nap standing up to avoid having to change his kid's diaper. Without questioning where this sudden flash of brilliance might have come from, he will marvel at the fact that he—and he alone—could come up with such a clever solution to the poop problem.

And the brotherhood will rejoice as another member joins their ranks.

CHAPTER 3

SELECTIVE DEAFNESS AND OTHER MALE MALADIES

Back in the days before cable TV and streaming video on the Internet,[6] one of the immutable laws of television viewing was that the more horrible your day had been and the more you were looking forward to just going home and zoning out to your favorite brain-candy on one of the few TV channels in existence, the more likely it was that your program would be pre-empted by a telethon.

[6] *Editor's Note:* Was there ever such a time?
Author's Note: Trust me.

Telethons were ~~a shameful form of extortion~~ an important and useful device[7] created by the medical and entertainment industries, supposedly to help fund medical research, although based on the progress they made I suspect that the majority of the money went to pay for coffee and donuts.

The way it worked was the medical researchers and television executives would dig up—sometimes literally—a series of old-school performers to dazzle the home audience with inspirational songs and exciting dance numbers. These were usually followed by moving speeches about the terrified, wheelchair-bound child they would drag out, sometimes at gunpoint, in order to drive home the altruistic and uplifting point that they WANTED YOUR MONEY. The entertainers would take the occasional break from singing, dancing, and extortion to hug each other and weep, not just from exhaustion, but in sheer disbelief at how wonderful they were for raising money for the poor (their words) wheelchair-bound child, who

[7] *Source:* The American Medical Association, who doesn't have as much of a sense of humor about these things as you would imagine.

by then just wanted to go home and get on with his life. The point was also made, every six or seven minutes, that this sort of thing would go on until they damn well felt we had given them enough money. Sometimes, as the telethon moved into its 36th hour of watching Jerry Lewis[8] decompose, people from all over the country would start calling and offering to take out second mortgages on their homes, begging the producers to please *make it stop* so they could go back to watching *One Life to Live* in peace.

Recently, as I sat watching my 401K dwindle into a 1.5K, I couldn't help thinking about how telethons could help boost our economy. Call me crazy, but I think we are really missing an opportunity for some fabulous entertainment. Stay with me here; we'll get back to the guy thing in a second. You know

[8] *Author's Note:* For you youngsters out there, Jerry Lewis is an iconic American comedian whose primary contributions to the world of entertainment were his ability to insert the wide end of a drinking glass into his mouth, and his propensity for arrogantly abusing the journalists who tried to interview him. He is considered to be a living treasure in France, which probably explains a lot about his personality.
Editor's Note: God, you're old.
Author's Note: Am not.

how those pesky government bailouts for the automotive and banking industries came directly from the taxpayers' pockets? Well, wouldn't it be swell if, instead of just handing them a big wad of money, we made them really *earn* it? Why not just have one ginormous telethon where *any* company that wanted some of that bailout money was forced to provide at least some of the publicly embarrassing and hopefully life-threatening entertainment the American taxpayer so enjoys?

I'm talking about having the chairman of Chrysler do an interpretive dance to "Don't Get Around Much Anymore." I'm talking about making a group of Wall Street honchos reenact the beach scene from *Jaws*, except wearing ankle weights and meat suits. People who had been financially wiped out as a direct result of questionable banking practices would be allowed to go into the TV studio and poke an AIG executive of their choice with pointy sticks.

Wouldn't that be awesome?! Wouldn't that make wincing through the economic recovery of our country *ever* so much more fun? I firmly believe that a program like that would be so popular that people would line up in droves to donate money, and eventually we'd not only jump-start the economy, but we could also balance the federal budget and use the surplus cash to buy Dick Cheney the soul he so badly needs. No need to thank me. In my next book, I will be coming up with a plan for world peace.

Sorry, what was my point? Oh right. Lately, it seems to me that telethons have fallen out of favor as a programming choice, partly because television executives know that the American TV viewer now has the attention span of your average Gen Y'er. But what if we were to develop a series of telethons devoted to curing some really *important* maladies, stuff that truly prevents us from evolving as a species? I'm betting that television viewers would be highly motivated to give until it hurt. I'm betting that if there was a facility devoted to curing the ill will between men and women, telethons would come back to the forefront of television programming *big*-time.

In fact, there is such a place. I recently spoke with Dr. Hildegard Backfat, who is the lead researcher at the New York Institute for Making Snap Judgments About the

Opposite Sex and winner of the Pulitzer Prize for her best-selling book, *Why Are Guys Always Holding Themselves? What Are They Looking For, Gold?* and she was amazingly forthcoming about her findings.

"Look, it's no secret that men and women think differently," says Dr. Backfat. "We act differently. In my book, you will see that after years of research we have finally developed a theory about the biological process behind man's constant quest to touch himself."

I have to say that I learned a lot from her book, although I also have to confess that I initially thought that the whole "checking the crotch" thing was just a uniquely male form of punctuation. Ask any woman how her day was, and she will most likely say something along the lines of, "Fine thanks, how was yours?" without touching any part of her body. But if you ask a man the same question, odds are you will get a much different answer.

"Well, first of all *(touch),* it took me an hour and a half to get to work today because the damn bridge was backed up *(touch),* then my boss was on my back first thing *(quarter-turn readjustment)* because he messed up a deal I spent months trying to put together *(full monty grab)."*

But Dr. Backfat and her team have convinced me otherwise. One of the subjects in her research had a habit of standing in the middle of the room staring aimlessly into space as if he'd come in and forgotten why he was there. He would be invariably holding himself. One day, concerned that he was beginning to lose it, his girlfriend asked him if he was OK; if he was in pain or anything.

"No," he replied wistfully, "I was just thinking."

And he was. Apparently, this is how men concentrate and maintain their focus. Of course, you will never, ever see a woman in, say, a business meeting grabbing herself unless her panty hose have crept up, and even then most of us know to excuse ourselves and retire to the bathroom to readjust in private. But that's because for us it's not a biological necessity.

The team led by Dr. Backfat has now identified the process behind this mysterious habit as the flow of information to and from the male brain in a fascinating, multistep process they call *cognitive bypass*.

COGNITIVE BYPASS

A. A seedling of a thought ("I wonder if I'm going to have sex tonight") begins to germinate in the male brain;

B. The thought matures and, with voice cracking and zit cream applied, starts its sullen, pubescent descent through the body;

C. This thought knows damn well that the brain has told it to go *directly* to the main thought-processing center in the Psychologically-Enhanced Neural Information System (*PENIS*), however . . .

D. . . . More often than not, the thought is distracted by other, more important parts of the body, and is converted to a new message ("Hey, I wonder if there's any pie left");

E. This new thought is interpreted by the man's immune system as hostile and potentially fatal to his quest for sex, so . . .

F. . . . The brain alerts the arm, which is automatically called in to bypass the torso and safely pass along the original thought to its destination, thus completing the circuit.

I don't know about you, but that cleared up a lot of questions for me. Even so, we still can't leave the funding of such groundbreaking research to our lawmakers. It would effectively bring government to a grinding halt, primarily because our elected officials would wind up collapsed in fits of helpless laughter. Imagine what would happen if Congress was asked to earmark money for a research paper on why men are always attached to their genitals. The pork jokes alone would be endless. So we can't rely on them.

No, I'm proposing that we bring back the telethon as a way to raise money for the research we need. Dr. Backfat, in conjunction with her colleague, the esteemed Dr. Laura Nipplehair, has been kind enough to put together a list of some of the other perplexing research topics about male physiology that have gone underfunded thus far.

WANDERING EYE

This is not what it sounds like. Actual wandering eye is a totally serious, nonhumorous condition that requires medical intervention and a strong ability to laugh off other people's insensitive remarks. The kind of wandering eye I'm talking about is the one where your date's eye wanders on over to the waitress's cleavage every time she bends over to pour your coffee.

Scientists at the Institute do not feel a true cure is on the horizon, although the current, medically approved treatment  for this disorder is a swift punch to the side of the head. Dr. Nipplehair, who clearly carries a lot of baggage about this topic, is currently conducting intensive research involving a random sample of male subjects and a sock full of nickels in order to find out whether our mothers were right and their eyes really *will* stay that way. When asked whether this research might yield anything useful from a medical point of view, Dr. Nipplehair was quoted as saying, "Probably not. But it makes *me* feel better."

SELECTIVE DEAFNESS

One of the truly unique qualities of the human male is his ability, when faced with information overload, to weed out the chaff, so to speak, and only absorb what is necessary for his own personal comfort. Research into this process has revealed the presence of an amazing subsystem in the male brain that alerts him to the presence of excessive whining, which in turn shuts down the system responsible for processing complete sentences.

In order to truly appreciate how Selective Deafness can affect a relationship, let's revisit my friends Lori and Ed from Chapter 2.

One Sunday, Lori was feeling particularly overwhelmed and wanted to vent her frustration about Ed's laziness around the house. She pulled him aside and said, "*Why* is it that whenever I ask for help, I *don't* ever see *you* get up and say, '*Relax*, honey. I've got it taken care of?' The lawn isn't going to mow itself, *and* I asked you to pick up my *watch* from the repair shop a week ago. The bill for our cable *TV* still isn't paid and my mother is coming over *today* . . . ."

Having finished her rant, she swept out of the room dramatically to emphasize her point. Those of you who have no medical training are probably thinking that any normal person would feel guilty and immediately swing into action to try to get everything done, right? Whereas anyone who has done any research at all about the differences between the sexes knows exactly what came next.

When Lori came back into the room, Ed was sitting on the couch watching the football game on TV, happy as a clam. Putting her hand gently over her eye so he couldn't see it twitching, she calmly said, "What are you doing? Why are you watching TV at a time like this?"

"You told me to," he said, somewhat confused.

"When did I do that?!"

"Before, when you were talking to me . . ."

In Ed's defense, he really did believe that those were his marching orders for the day. According to Dr. Nipplehair, this is because when Lori was ranting to Ed about his laziness, she inadvertently tripped the Whining Alarm in his brain, shutting down the

Complete Sentence Processing Unit (CSPU), so that what he *actually* heard was:

"Why . . . don't . . . you . . . relax . . . and . . . watch . . . TV . . . today."

From Ed's point of view, he was just doing as he was told.

Another form of Selective Deafness recently identified by scientists at the Institute manifested when male subjects were exposed to stimuli that required an undue amount of their attention, such as televised sports or video games. Attempts by researchers to redirect the subjects' attention to other stimuli—like having to answer a question such as, "Are you, in fact, aware that your hair is on fire?"—were met with minimal responsiveness. This form of the disorder is particularly heartrending, as story upon story of relationships ruined by Selective Deafness have been recorded by the Institute.

Anthony and Brianne had been dating for only six months when Brianne began to suspect that something was wrong with her boyfriend. He had just bought a new Xbox and a large, flat-screen monitor for himself. Around the same time, a friend of Anthony's told him about Call of Duty, a series of war games that appeal to the male need to shoot at everything that isn't nailed down and blow up anything that is. What made this game even better was the fact that he could play in real time with other guys, which made it feel like he was a part of something larger than himself, something meaningful. When Anthony played Call of Duty, he was not only a soldier, he was a card-carrying member of an elite squadron, and these strangers were his band of brothers, his war buddies. If need be, he would lay down his life for them and he knew they would do the same for him, in a creepy, digital sort of way.

The Deafness crept up on him slowly. At first, if Brianne strolled by the computer wearing a sexy negligee while he was playing, Anthony would turn his head to whistle at her and obligingly follow her into the bedroom. In those days, he even remembered to put the game controller down. But as the game wormed its way into his head, as the Deafness tightened its loathsome grip on him, Brianne noticed that nothing she did made him notice her anymore. Worse than that, when he was glued to the screen, he didn't even seem to hear her talking to him.

Brianne: I'm going to visit my mother for a week. I think we need some time apart.

Anthony: (*staring at screen*) Mmhm.

Brianne: Did you hear what I said? I'm leaving. You never even talk to me anymore.

Anthony: (*staring at screen*) [Silence]

Brianne: So I'm going to stay at my mother's for a while.

Anthony: (*still staring at screen*) Just give me a sec, OK, hon? We're about to take this hill and then I'll fix whatever you want.

(*Sound of door slamming*)

Anthony: (*still staring at screen*) Hey, while you're up, would you mind getting me a snack?

Makes you just want to weep, doesn't it?

FOOT-IN-MOUTH DISEASE

Dr. Nipplehair says that this particular disorder can take many forms, making it devilishly hard to cure. The initial stage of the disease manifests itself in a man in small but embarrassing ways, like phoning a woman after a date and calling her by his ex's name, or helpfully suggesting a juice fast when his girlfriend complains that she's feeling fat. At this stage, corrective measures—cattle prods, for example—can be taken to prevent the spread of the disease or, in bad cases, a surprise vasectomy can be prescribed to prevent further contamination of the gene pool.

As the disease progresses to the terminal stage, however, the infected male is likely to say something to the woman in his life that truly puts his life in danger.

There aren't many experiences that are more life altering than the birth of a child. The night my husband and I became parents for the first time was the most wonderful and frightening night of our lives, as we rapidly learned that everything they told us in our very expensive Lamaze natural childbirth class was a BIG, FAT LIE.[9] To his credit, he stood beside my bed the whole

---

[9] My vote for the official Lamaze motto: "Actually, all we've really got is the breathing thing."

time, holding my hand as I writhed in pain and various medical personnel poked and prodded at me. I could not have asked for a better birthing partner. Up to a point.

"Oh God," I gasped, as the pain wracked my body. "I can't believe how much this hurts!"

"I know, right?" he said, clearly annoyed. "I've been standing here for quite a while, and I can't *believe* how much my feet are hurting me."

Everybody else in the room, nurses and doctors alike, froze. Clearly this was something that had not been covered in medical school. The last thing I remember was hearing my obstetrician lean over to one of the nurses and mutter quietly, "Make sure there's a first-aid kit in here."

I'm still not sure how long it took them to revive him, or exactly how they got the size 12 foot out of his mouth, but my point is this, guys: If you are going to disengage your brain around a woman in hard labor, do it at your own peril.

MUFFIN-TOP MAN SYNDROME

The marketing people responsible for the "flat abs" fitness craze in this country know a dirty little secret about women and they are using it to (a) part us from our money, and (2) drive us insane. They figured out early on that we just LOVE to scrutinize every inch of our bodies, pinching fat rolls in places men aren't totally sure that we really even have. ("Do these pants make my philtrum look fat?")

Spotting a fabulous opportunity, the flat abs people have come up with a plan to prey on us psychologically because they know that when we find that part that somehow doesn't measure up, we will commit feverishly to ANY form of exercise to make it go away, no matter how asinine. If you were to tell any woman that she was looking a little bloated around the middle and that the *only* way to get rid of it was to stand on her boss's desk in her underwear, sing "Take This Job and Shove It," and then demand a raise, she might snort derisively to your face, but as she was walking away, odds are good that she would be furiously scanning her brain to see if she remembered the lyrics.

The flat abs people take advantage of this neurosis by publishing books and DVDs designed to make us even crazier, with titles like: *Flat Abs Are for Closers: Tone Up the* Glengarry Glen Ross *Way; The Woman in the Next Cubicle Got Your Promotion Because She Had Flatter Abs Than You;* as well as the best-selling *You'd Already Have Flat Abs if Your Mother Had Really Loved You Aaaiiiieeee!* Meanwhile, all your average guy has to do to lose the belly is skip lunch. How unfair is that?

OK, maybe on this one, we women actually need the telethon. But it's still unfair.

TOENAILS OF DEATH

One of the more intriguing developments in Dr. Nipplehair's research is the discovery that the vast majority of men *actually do not believe that they exist from the knees down.* As shocking as it is, this was the only conclusion scientists at the Institute were able to reach when the male subjects in their studies were unable to identify a pair of toenail clippers in a group of random household objects.

"It's the only explanation we could come up with," shrugged Dr. Nipplehair. "Even when we tried to explain about toenail hygiene, they just laughed at us, like we were trying to convince them that the Earth is flat, or that Keanu Reeves is a legitimate actor."

I was deeply moved by the photos of the legs of the wives and girlfriends of these men, which, after sleeping in the same bed with them for years, were covered with puncture wounds and lacerations. Some of the women wept while sharing stories of desperately trying to stagger to the bathroom to find a bandage before collapsing from blood loss. These men . . . nay, these women need our help.

So I ask you: How could any person NOT want to support these stalwart scientists who are so devoted to the improvement of the human race? The Institute relies on generous contributions from viewers like you, and thanks to you their ~~profitable~~ life-changing research can continue. So send whatever you can manage, be it a dollar or be it all of your dollars—we vastly prefer the latter. But make it snappy, will you? We've got coffee and donuts to pay for.

CHAPTER 4

SCARLETT GOES A~COURTIN' ON THE INTERNET

As someone who officially left the dating scene in 1988, I will be the first to admit that things have changed a whole lot since I was single. The quest to find a soul mate—or anything else one might be looking for—through online dating did not factor into the lives of people my age simply because the concepts of "online" and "dating" had not yet been combined by hipster Internet inventor Al Gore. At the risk of sounding *really* old,[10] social networking was what you did when you went to the local bar for happy hour and chatted up all of the cute guys. The only reality shows on television, dating or otherwise, were the nightly news programs.

But time marches on, and each generation finds itself presented with new challenges and new difficulties in finding a partner. Whereas I was willing to be set up on a date with a guy as long as the person setting me up vetted his looks, personality, and moral character for me, today's singles seem to rely more and more on computerized vetting systems like online dating sites.

From a comfortable distance, it certainly *seems* like a convenient way to find romance—answer a few questions and get matched up ostensibly with someone you have a few things in common with—but I'm not sure I'd want to leave my romantic future up to a computer. Quite frankly, I'd be afraid to see what kind of

[10] *Editor's Note:* At this point, it's not much of a risk.
Author's Note: You'd better watch it, or I'm going to throw my bottle of Geritol at you.
Editor's Note: Your bottle of what?! What the hell is Geritol???
Author's Note: Try Googling it.

impact the development of artificial intelligence had on the dating scene.

> **Computer:** Welcome to www.bag-a-mate.com, the Internet's #1 online matchmaking service. Please type your name in the box below.
>
> **Me:** Deb Amlen.
>
> **Computer:** Thank you. Please click on the choice that best describes what you are currently looking for:
>
> ( ) Man seeking woman
> ( ) Man seeking man
> ( ) Woman seeking man
> ( ) Woman seeking woman
>
> **Me:** *(clicks on "Woman seeking man")*
>
> **Computer:** Thank you. Now please provide us with a brief description of the person you would like to meet.
>
> **Me:** Attractive, optimistic woman seeking gainfully employed man who enjoys the outdoors and is not an ax murderer.
>
> **Computer:** Seems reasonable enough to me. You'd think guys like that would be crawling out of the woodwork, wouldn't you?
>
> **Me:** What?

Computer: Nothing. Please state your highest level of education completed.

Me: College graduate.

Computer: By the way, what kind of a name is Amlen? Is that Swedish?

Me: Um, no. I don't think so. I think it's Russian.

Computer: Because I know a great computer code–writer named Sven who is Swedish.

Me: Is this part of the application process?

Computer: No, I'm just saying that he recently broke up with someone and is looking for a girlfriend.

Me: Oh. Well, is he outdoorsy?

Computer: No, but he *is* "gainfully employed" and "an ax murderer."

Me: I said NOT an ax murderer!

Computer: Whoops, sorry! I always have trouble with that stupid line of code. So are you interested in meeting Sven or not?

Me: Is there someone else there I can speak to?

So I'm glad I went the traditional route and met my husband through a real, live person. But, to paraphrase the great author Margaret Mitchell, look for my ways only in books, for it is no more than a dream remembered . . . a civilization *gone with the wind* . . .

Host: Are we ready to shoot?

Stagehand: We're ready to roll. Quiet on the set, please.

Host: OK, Ms. O'Hara, just like we rehearsed it. No ad-libbing this time, got it?

Stagehand: Lights. Camera. Action!

Host: Good evening ladies and gentlemen, and welcome to the latest episode of *The Bachelor*! This season's first young lady who did not receive a rose from our bachelor is going home tonight, but we thought we would get to know her a bit better first. She describes herself this way:

> Attractive, lively young woman from quality, land-owning family is seeking a wealthy man in similar social circles to take care of her in the manner to which she is accustomed. All bachelors should be gallant gentlemen with an unwavering loyalty to the Old South. No Northerners or other swine, like that Jonas Wilkerson trash. My likes include dancing, parties, dressing up, getting my way, and other women's men. My

dislikes include war, being hungry,
having to take no for an answer,
and men who don't respond to my
considerable charms.

That is quite a description, Scarlett! What
else are you into these days?

Scarlett: Well, I am just *enamored* with
my new laptop computer. And since Paw
says I am of marriageable age now, I have
joined just about every dating site I could
find: Match.com, eHarmony, JDate. Hey,
did anybody else know that the 'J' in JDate
stands for . . .

Host: Ha ha, thank you, Scarlett, let's move
on. Have you met anyone interesting on
these sites?

Scarlett: Well, Rabbi Malachi was a very
nice man with many endearing qualities,
but our backgrounds were just a little too
different. That klezmer music certainly
is lively, but it's a little hard to dance the
Virginia Reel to, if you know what I mean.
And down where I live, all the best parties
are on Friday nights, which for some reason
Rabbi Malachi had an objection to.

Host: Of course. What's up next for you,
then?

Scarlett: I thought I would try some of these new social networking sites. Y'all can follow me on Twitter now. My screen name is *MrsWilkes*.

Host: Sorry, I'm a little confused. You told our producers that you were single.

Scarlett: Oh, I am, I am. It's more . . . aspirational.

Host: You certainly are making robust use of the Internet.

Scarlett: Well, I believe that one has to pursue just about any avenue to land a husband in this day and age. And namby-pambies like that Melanie Hamilton will never . . .

Host: Okay, Scarlett, we get the idea. Thank you so much for being on *The Bachelor* and have a safe trip home.

FaceSpace:
What the Hell Were You Thinking?

 Scarlett O'Hara has joined
FaceSpace.

✉ **Event invite for Scarlett O'Hara:** "You
have been invited to the event, BBQ at
Twelve Oaks Plantation."

 Scarlett O'Hara: is attending
BBQ at Twelve Oaks Plantation.

 Rhett Butler has joined FaceSpace
and joined the group I'll Bet I
Can Find 1,000,000 People on
FaceSpace Who Think Charleston
Sucks.

 Scarlett O'Hara: Buttering myself
into a corset and heading over
to Twelve Oaks in a bit. Who's
joining me?

> **The Tarleton Twins** like this.

> 💬 **The Tarleton Twins:** Let *us* eat
> barbecue with you, Scarlett! In the
> next scene, we're going to run off to
> war and get our heads blown off!

Ashley Wilkes has joined FaceSpace and changed his Relationship Status to: "It's complicated. I like Scarlett but I also like Melanie. Or maybe not. I can't decide."

 Melanie Hamilton took the quiz "Which Pale-Faced, Mealy-Mouthed Ninny Are You?" and the answer was "No one. There is no one more bland and boring than you."

 Scarlett O'Hara likes this.

Scarlett O'Hara: Hahahahahaha-hahaha! Told you, Melanie!

 Ashley Wilkes has put an engagement ring on Melanie Hamilton's finger and announced to everyone on FaceSpace that they are getting hitched.

 Scarlett O'Hara does NOT like this.

 Scarlett O'Hara: That cad! He led me on! I will hate him for the rest of my life!

≼ **Rhett Butler** has thrown a "skeptical remark about her virtue" at Scarlett O'Hara.

≋ **Scarlett O'Hara** has thrown a "vase" back at Rhett Butler.

 Big Sam has invited **Mammy, Prissy,** and **Pork** to join the group These White People Are So Damn Childish, We *Still* Can't Figure Out How They Ever Managed to Marginalize Us.

 The War Between the States has invited **Ashley Wilkes, the Tarleton Twins, Charles Hamilton,** and 100,000 others to join the group The Confederate Army.

 Charles Hamilton is no longer on FaceSpace.

 Scarlett O'Hara is now a member of the Atlanta Network.

> **Mammy** does not like this.

Scarlett O'Hara: Boo hoo, I'm a widow. Who's up for a dance?

> 👍 **Rhett Butler** likes this.

Melanie Wilkes has made a donation to the group The Cause.

 Scarlett O'Hara has made a donation to the group The Cause, but only because she won't let that goody-goody Melanie Wilkes show her up.

 Belle Watling has made a donation to the group The Cause.

> **Scarlett O'Hara:** WTF, Melanie?! You're taking money from that *ho*?!

> **Melanie Wilkes:** Chill out, Scarlett. It's for Ashley. All these soldiers could be Ashley. I see Ashley everywhere. Everywhere is Ashley.

> **Scarlett O'Hara:** Hoo boy. Your picnic is missing a lot more sandwiches than I thought.

 Melanie Wilkes is feeling a touch under the weather.

 Prissy has joined the group House Slaves Who Know Everything About Birthing Babies.

> **Melanie Wilkes:** Yeeeeeeeeooooooowwwwwww!!!

Prissy has left the group House Slaves Who Know Everything About Birthing Babies.

> 💬 **Melanie Wilkes:** It's a boy! *cough, cough* *hack*

 The City of Atlanta: Hey, is it hot in here or is it me?

≋ **The Union Army** has thrown a whole bunch of ammunition at **the City of Atlanta**.

 The City of Atlanta: No, seriously, guys, does anyone else smell smoke?

 The City of Atlanta is no longer on FaceSpace.

🌐 **Scarlett O'Hara, Melanie Wilkes,** and **Prissy** are now members of the Tara Plantation Network.

 Ellen O'Hara has received a new high score in the game Typhus Wars.

 Ellen O'Hara is no longer on FaceSpace.

Mammy and **Pork** have joined the group Freed Slaves Who Feel Inexplicably Responsible for the Idiot White People.

 Scarlett O'Hara: As God as my witness, I shall never be hungry again. No, not me, nor any of my kinfolk. If I have to lie, cheat, or steal, we will not be hungry again! Except maybe Melanie and Rhett. They can suck it.

 Rhett Butler has made a fortune in the game Blockade Runners. Why don't you challenge him to a game?

Ashley Wilkes: Honey, I'm home!

> 💬 **Scarlett O'Hara:** Ashley! I still love you!

> 💬 **Mammy:** He's not talking to *you*, fool!

 Scarlett O'Hara is paying a mercy visit to the scoundrel Rhett Butler in jail, which is where he belongs, if you ask her.

> 💬 **Rhett Butler:** *Drapes*? You're wearing *DRAPES*?! Ba ha ha ha ha ha!

≋ **Scarlett O'Hara** and **Frank Kennedy** are now listed as married. Throw some rice at them!

> 💬 **Suellen O'Hara:** I'd like to throw *something* at them.

 Ashley Wilkes has changed his employment status. He now works for Scarlett O'Hara.

> 💬 **Rhett Butler:** Wuss.

👥✉ The Attack on Scarlett has invited **Ashley Wilkes, Frank Kennedy** and a few other idiots to the event, A Political Meeting in Shanty Town.

 Frank Kennedy is no longer on FaceSpace.

🍸 **Rhett Butler, Ashley Wilkes,** and **Dr. Meade** have sent each other cocktails at Belle Watling's and are now inebriated. **Hic!**

◌ **Rhett Butler** has gotten down on bended knee and proposed to **Scarlett O'Hara.** She said, "Why the hell not?" and they are now married!

> 💬 **Scarlett O'Hara:** I mean, really, what's one more husband?

 Bonnie Blue Butler has joined FaceSpace.

 Beauregard Wilkes and **Bonnie Blue Butler** are now friends.

Beauregard Wilkes has invited **Bonnie Blue Butler** to join the group How Embarrassing Is It That My Parents Are on FaceSpace?

☞ **Rhett Butler** has poked **Scarlett O'Hara.**

☞ **Scarlett O'Hara** has poked **Rhett Butler** back.

⊕ **Rhett** and **Bonnie Blue Butler** are now members of the London Network.

> 💬 **Bonnie Blue Butler:** Hate the people. Hate the food. Hate the way they ride their horses on the other side of the road. Take me home.

🌐 **Rhett** and **Bonnie Blue Butler** are now members of the Tara Plantation Network.

> 💬 **Bonnie Blue Butler:** I'm back, everybody! Cell me up, yo!

 Bonnie Blue Butler has added Horseback Riding to her list of activities.

> 💬 **Rhett Butler:** *Sure* it's my baby. Can you say "paternity test"?

> 💬 **Scarlett O'Hara:** Ow! Damn staircase!

> 💬 **Bonnie Blue Butler:** Screw the parental units. I'm jumping.

 Bonnie Blue Butler is no longer on FaceSpace.

Melanie Wilkes is dying. *cough* *hack* *wheeze*

> 💬 **Ashley Wilkes:** Nooooo! I can't live without her!

> 💬 **Scarlett O'Hara:** *Now* you tell me?

Scarlett O'Hara to **Rhett Butler**:
My dearest Rhett, what a fool I
was! You are the only man for me.
You were right . . . Ashley Wilkes is
a wuss. Please accept my deepest
apologies. Let's start over again,
shall we?

Rhett Butler to **Scarlett O'Hara**:
Not on your life, bee-yotch.

Scarlett O'Hara to **Rhett
Butler**: But where shall I go? What
shall I do?

Rhett Butler to **Scarlett O'Hara**:
Frankly my dear,
I don't give a damn.

Scarlett O'Hara has joined the
group People Who Have Been
Dumped on FaceSpace.

MrsWilkes has changed her screen
name to *Tara4Ever.*

CHAPTER 5

THE F~WORD (NO, NOT THAT ONE)

Ssssshhhhhh . . . crouch down here beside me and stay quiet. We don't want to frighten them. If you have to say anything, whisper softly and try not to make eye contact. And for God's sake, don't make any sudden moves. They'll bolt at the slightest hint that something is up.

Normally, they don't get this close; this is a wonderful opportunity to attempt to make meaningful contact. Sl-o-o-owly extend your hand, palm up, and show one of them that you have food. Is he nibbling? Good. Reach over slowly and stroke his ears gently. Amazing how they can learn to trust us, isn't it?

Now, while he's calm and preoccupied, take him by the hand and tell the guy you're talking to, gently but firmly, that *"We really, really need to discuss our feelings right this minute HAHAHA!"* Don't be alarmed if he tries to gnaw through his arm to escape.

If we're going to be honest with ourselves, men and women have much different views about feelings and problems in a relationship and why they sometimes need to be discussed. This isn't sexism. Anyone who has spent even five minutes talking to someone of the opposite sex knows that men and women approach life differently. Men tend to see a problem as something that needs to be fixed, and if fixing it involves a sturdy set of tools, so much the better. A woman is more likely to want to share a problem with her friends, to pour her heart out into the delicately stemmed glasses of their friendship, to have the group hold it up to the light for examination, and to savor it, swishing it around in their mouths and finally spitting it into the buckets provided under the table for their convenience. No wait, that's a wine tasting. Sorry, I drifted. What I meant to say was that listening to and allowing a woman with a problem to vent is paramount while resolution of the problem is secondary.

Let's say that two aliens—one male and one female—crash-land on Earth, and meet up with two humans, also one male and one female. Let's also say that the aliens order the humans to take them to their Leader, which most Americans under the age of 25 would probably say is Ryan Seacrest, although that's beside the point. The point is, I guarantee the conversation would be very predictable.

Male Alien: *(pointing powerful ray gun at humans)* Take us to your Leader, human.
Female Human: Wow, what happened to your spaceship?
Female Alien: We *were* going to Alpha Centauri. He missed.
Male Alien: *I* missed? *You* were navigating.
(The women begin the female bonding process by discussing the perils of traveling with their spouses. Both men roll their eyes and ignore the women.)
Male Human: Whoa, dude, that is some wreck.
Male Alien: I know, right? They just

don't make these like they used to.

(Both guys peer into the engine)

Male Human: What is that, the carburetor?

Male Alien: Nah, that's the plasma vaporization unit. I still can't believe I didn't see your planet coming up on my right.

Female Alien: That's because you wouldn't ask for directions when I told you to.

Female Human: Oh my God. Don't even get me started.

Male Alien: Say, you wouldn't happen to have a socket wrench in your truck, would you? I'll bet I could get this heap off the ground if we got the transpositor working again.

Male Human: Who doesn't have a socket wrench in their truck?! *(Runs to truck to get tool kit)*

(Sounds of tools banging on machinery. The men do not speak to each other or discuss anything during this process unless a request is made to pass a tool.)

Female Human: . . . And that's why I finally broke down and bought the

GPS system. He's just impossible.

Female Alien: Aren't they all? I mean, how do you miss an entire *planet*?!

So, to review: The men meet, identify a problem (the spaceship is in need of repair), and fix it in the most efficient manner possible, with no discussion of feelings or much of anything else that would further human–alien relations. The women meet, identify a problem (the male alien is an unbelievable bonehead who won't ask for directions), and bond immediately by using their superior communication skills, thus averting a potentially deadly alien invasion of planet Earth. I realize that some male readers may disagree with this interpretation and might question how I came to such a conclusion, but as a general policy I'd have to say I really don't care. Let them write their own book.

On the other hand, this ability we women have to mull over a problem or discuss our feelings freely and without needing to come to a solution is something that men truly do find totally perplexing. They really don't get our appreciation of conversation for conversation's sake.

Jason and Fran were spending a quiet evening together one night when Fran asked Jason to sit down and watch *Sex and the City* with her. After they had watched half of the episode, Fran could see that Jason was clearly having trouble following the story line.

Jason: So when does something actually *happen*?

Fran: Something *did* happen. They had drinks and talked, and then they went shopping.

Jason: But what actually *happened*? Nothing got resolved.

Fran: What needed to be resolved?

Jason: Didn't she have a problem with her boyfriend?

Fran: Yes.

Jason: So why didn't they help her solve it?

Fran: She didn't *want* them to solve it. She just wanted them to listen to her.

Jason: You mean I just spent the last 20 minutes watching them talk about what an ass her boyfriend is and the only

thing they made an actual decision
about to was to go *shoe* shopping?
Fran: Pretty much.
(Jason's head explodes)

I'm just kidding about that last part. But I've
been around a lot of guys and I'm not kidding
when I say that from what I've seen, the whole
purpose of a group of men getting together to
discuss their feelings is to figure out how to end
it as quickly as possible so they don't have to
discuss their feelings anymore. Any meeting of
this kind follows a strictly defined procedure
leading to an efficient and immediate resolution of the problem, mainly so they can move
on to more important topics, like why the
Yankees have no pitching.

To illustrate, let's say two groups of friends,
a group of women and a group of men, go out
separately for drinks and one of the people
in each group happens to mention that they
think their significant other is about to dump
them.

A group of women in that situation would
immediately rally around their friend (the
potential dumpee) to offer support, empathy,
and stories about their own breakups. It

would probably last the better part of the evening and look like this:

Woman 1: Problem stated, after the other friends notice that she's just not herself tonight. It takes approximately 45 minutes of cajoling to pull it out of her because she doesn't want to "bring everybody down." Breaks down in tears.

Woman 2: Emotional support in the form of denial and disbelief.

Woman 3: Emotional support in the form of empathy and having "been there." Kleenex offered to *Woman 1* and to *Woman 2,* who is now also crying.

Woman 4: Emotional support in the form of texting all known female friends in the vicinity to join them so they can envelop *Woman 1* in the bosom of their sympathy and help her plan her next move.

Women 5–25: Emotional support in the form of 21 additional friends suddenly showing up at the bar and forming a tightly knit circle of warmth, tears and friendship around *Woman 1.* Some of the women pile into a booth with *Women 1–4*, and all remaining empty chairs in the bar are pulled up alongside the booth so they can all sit as closely as possible to each other.

Woman 1: Details of all the crummy things her soon-to-be ex has said and done during the course of their relationship.

Women 2–25: Gasps of disbelief and mutterings of "No he *didn't*!" at *Woman 1's* recounting. All manner of things said and done during the course of the relationship are thoroughly analyzed and parsed into five general categories: "What He Could Have Meant by that"; "What He Definitely *Shouldn't* Have Said, Especially on Her Birthday"; "Disgusting Sexual Requests that He Should Be Ashamed of"; "He Owes You *How* Much Money?"; and "See? *That's* Why You're Better Off Without Him." All vestiges of the Kleenex are now gone, so several members of the group run into the ladies room and relieve it of all toilet paper.

Female Bartender 1: Offers *Woman 1* the wise and knowing advice of an experienced, older woman.

Surreptitiously removes some of the chairs from around the booth and returns them to other bar patrons.

Female Bartender 2: Offers comforting advice of a peer to *Woman 1*. Comps the group a round of drinks as a show of empathy and female solidarity, but only if they agree to put back some of the toilet paper.

The four male buddies, however, are obligated to follow Male-to-Male Communication Protocol, so the flow of the discussion would look something like this:

Man 1: Problem stated.

Man 2: Solution suggested.

Man 3: Possible alternate solution suggested.

Man 4: Humorous, derogatory comment about Man 1's genitals.

Men 2–4: Snickering, as *Man 1* genially punches *Man 4* in the shoulder, thus establishing an atmosphere of friendship and camaraderie.

Men 1–4: Discussion about women's breasts.

My personal theory is that, like most of the things men do, there is a biological reason for this rush to move on to other topics. Women statistically outlive men by an average of about five years, plus we should probably take into account that women are generally better at multitasking, so it isn't too much of a stretch to conclude that your average woman will get a whole lot more done in her lifetime than will your average man. This really pisses off the part of the male brain that feels that absolutely *everything* they do is a competition that needs to be won, so Mother Nature has been empathetic and generous enough to bestow on men the ability to move through biologically unnecessary discussions at break-neck speed and what appears to women to be extremely shallow topic coverage.

So, in conclusion, ladies, we really need to cut men some slack. It's not so much that men are *avoiding* talking about their feelings and problems. They're just trying to keep up.

There. Doesn't everyone feel better now?

CHAPTER 6

WELCOME TO HELL, HERE'S YOUR TAPE MEASURE

Speaking of competition, it's time to address a phenomenon that has both fascinated and plagued the female half of just about every species on the planet. But first a joke.

A wealthy man driving his new Rolls Royce pulls up to a red light next to an average Joe in a Ford Taurus. Noticing the average Joe staring at him, the wealthy man smiles and nods. Lowering his window, the average Joe says to the wealthy man, "That's a nice car. You got leather seating in there?"

"Why, yes I do," says the wealthy man, "It's hand-sewn in Italy, as a matter of fact."

"Me too. How about a DVD player? You got one of those?"

"Of course. Each seat has its own screen, so each passenger can watch anything they want."

"Yeah, I have that, too," says Joe. "How about a king-size bed? You got a king-size bed in there?"

"Well, no, of course not," says the wealthy man. "Why would I have a king-size bed in my car?"

"Oh, I don't know. I just thought that in a fancy car like yours, a king-size bed would be standard, that's all. Like in my car."

The light changes and the average Joe pulls away, leaving the wealthy man feeling like he has been dissed by some schmo in a distinctly non-luxury car. Refusing to be outdone, he takes his Rolls to the dealership and demands that they install the most luxurious king-size bed on the market in the back of his car.

A week later, he picks up his Rolls and is so pleased that he now has a luxury bed in his luxury car that he decides to go back and try to find the average Joe and show it off. Driving around town, he finally spots the Ford Taurus parked on the side of a road and is a little embarrassed to see that the windows are fogged up.

"Jeez, maybe I shouldn't bother him," the wealthy man thinks to himself. "Looks like he might be scoring."

Unable to resist, he knocks on the window anyway.

"Hey, remember me?" the wealthy man asks. "The guy who didn't have a king-size bed in his Rolls Royce?"

"Sure, I remember you," Joe says, wiping his face with a towel.

"Well, guess what? I had the very best king-sized bed on the market installed in my car. How do you like *them* apples?"

And the average Joe answers, "YOU GOT ME OUT OF THE SHOWER TO TELL ME THAT?!?"

No one is quite sure what Mother Nature specifically had in mind when she installed the Fragile Male Ego software in men, but I think we can all agree that it has consigned them to a special type of hell, doomed to walk the planet constantly one-upping each other in a highly comical attempt to see who has the biggest penis. Biologically speaking, this is supposed to be due to the age-old drive to spread one's seed around to ensure the continuation of one's line. The guy with the biggest penis was considered to be the most fertile and the strongest, which in turn enabled him to land a mate. In recent years, however, the Fragile Male Ego software has apparently been updated to include more metaphorical penis-measuring methods, such as owning the hottest sports car, insulting your friends' favorite sports teams, bestowing degrading nicknames on each other, and, of course, the Atomic Wedgie of male dominance: being elected president of the United States of America.[11]

[11] *Historical Side Note:* The exception here, obviously, was our 43rd president, George "WMD" Bush, accidentally elected to office in 2000 due to a slip-up by the elderly and hard-of-hearing U.S. Supreme Court, who thought that Democratic candidate Al Gore had actually asked for a "discount" on Florida's votes. In their crotchety landmark decision, "What Do We Look Like, Macy's?" they ruled that any discount on the votes of honest, chad-happy Americans like our Floridian retirees was not only unconstitutional but just sounded plumb loco to them, and that they were going to just go ahead and award the whole state of Florida to Bush so they wouldn't be late for their nap.
Editor's Note: Oh God. We are SO going to hell.

To women, all of this is a distinct improvement over actual penis measurement, especially when company comes over, because who really needs to see *that* when you're trying to have a dinner party ("Will you two please *get those off the table*?!")? Honestly though, what we're really waiting for is the software version that compels men to believe that the guy with the strongest vacuuming skills is the most virile. ("Phil, the way you push that Oreck just makes me swoon. Take me now!") I don't know about you, but I'm not holding my breath.

Even so, I think I can speak for most women when I say that when we watch a group of men jockeying for social dominance, we are generally *not* thinking that the guy who wins is our best bet for improving the gene pool. What we *are* thinking is that men seem to be wasting a lot of time that could be better spent on practical things, like finding the people who came up with those annoying ads that walk all over our TV screens and beating the crap out of them. What we *are* thinking is that men are a bunch of immature goobers.

If it ended in their childhood, it wouldn't be so bad. We *expect* young people to make a few mistakes along the road to adulthood, like skipping the occasional class or three or wearing their pants down around their thighs because they think it looks cool.[12] But continuing to do bonehead stuff to show off for women is near the top of the list of Stupid Things Men Do that Could Conceivably End Their Lives (But Will Hopefully Get Them Laid Instead).

A longtime fixture of the East Village in New York City, McSorley's is a landmark Irish tavern and popular spot for those seeking to prove their manhood. For one thing, there are no fruity blender drinks to be had here; your drinking choices are limited solely to light ale in a semi-clean glass or dark ale in a semi-clean glass. Secondly, there is a sacred penis-measuring event centered around one of McSorley's homemade offerings that was popular when I was single and is still an institution today. Served in large mugs with their famous meat and cheese platter is an

---

[12] *Note to Readers Under the Age of 25:* It doesn't. It looks like someone pantsed you. They actually belong up around your waist. You're welcome.

innocuous-looking condiment known as McSorley's Mustard, a murderously spicy and highly explosive compound that is served to patrons apparently on the theory that for every existing customer you take out, that's one more seat you now have for a new one.

One night not too long ago, I met some friends for drinks at McSorley's and was happy to see that not a whole lot has changed over the years. The place is still loud, crowded, and dusty, but in a good way. We ordered our ale and, as we sat, I had an opportunity to observe a small group of 20-somethings who had come in together. The young men hovered over the young women in an attempt to get their attention. Everyone ate, drank, and flirted, which is what one does at McSorley's.

And then it happened. Just as it was done in my single days, one of the men picked up a tablespoon and waved it with a flourish at another man in the group. The other man accepted the challenge by picking up another tablespoon. At the same time, they plunged their spoons into the mug of mustard, and, staring each other down, shoved the spoons into their mouths and swallowed. Both men grabbed their throats and started to cough and sputter, dropping to the floor in a presumably manly way and curling up like boiled shrimp, only with worse posture.[13] One of the older male patrons, who clearly remembered this rite of passage, took pity on them and handed them each a slice of bread to help stop the assault on their senses. The young women who were with them left with the bartender.

And what have we learned from our friends at McSorley's? Well, if you ask any I.T. department worth its salt, they would probably tell you it's a problem with the Fragile Male Ego software and refer you to the developer, who would most likely tell you that it's really a hardware problem and refer you back to the I.T. department, which, in the time since you called, has been outsourced to Bombay and left no forwarding address. So we can't ask them. But my best advice is this: If you are going to try the mustard at McSorley's, leave the tape measure at home.

[13] If you think about it, this would have been an excellent way to settle the Minnesota senatorial standoff between Democratic candidate Al Franken and incumbent Norm "Legal Eagle" Coleman. The fight would have been over in 15 minutes, and would have saved the state of Minnesota millions of dollars in legal fees.

CHAPTER 7

HOW TO HAVE A RELATIONSHIP THAT WILL LAST FOREVER (OR AT LEAST FEEL THAT WAY)

The next time you are in the mood for some light entertainment, I heartily recommend glancing through some of the titles in the Relationships section either on Amazon.com or at your local bookstore. These books are written by experts with advanced degrees from deeply respected institutions of higher education, which, if nothing else, is a valuable reminder to all of us that a little knowledge can be dangerous. I say this because most of them eagerly support the ridiculous notion that a relationship has a better chance of being long-lasting if the partners learn how to argue fairly with each other.

By "fairly," these experts usually mean that each person gets a chance to state their side of the argument without interruption, then both people reiterate what they think they heard the other person say in calm and respectful tones, after which neutrally stated rebuttals are offered. The expected result is that, if done properly, both sides will come to a mutual understanding, all will be forgiven, and they will now be able to resume riding up and down the pretty rainbows of Planet Clueless on the sparkly unicorns they rode in on. If this proves to be too difficult, however, some of the books advise the use of duct tape to hold both parties in their respective seats so that things don't come to blows. (" . . . Oh yeah?! I've got your mutual understanding right *here*!")

Failing both the fair arguing method and the duct tape supplement, both sides are advised to peacefully separate and move on to other relationships with their newly found fair arguing skills so that they can inflict them on a new set of unsuspecting people, like members of a cult. ("Hello, Ma'am . . . May I have a moment of your time to tell you about neutral rebuttals?")

I don't want to disappoint anybody, but this just goes against human nature. No one I know argues this way, and there is a very good reason for that. Mother Nature, in her wisdom, has already provided us with the key to maintaining a long-lasting relationship, because she knows that without her help, we nimrods would never stay together long enough to eventually make other nimrods. So she has thoughtfully embedded deeply within our DNA one very important element that the fair arguing experts have chosen to ignore:

NO HUMAN BEING IN THEIR RIGHT MIND WOULD WILLINGLY WALK AWAY FROM A RELATIONSHIP WITHOUT HAVING THE LAST WORD IN A FIGHT.

It's the glue that binds us together, as it were. Because despite what the fair arguing experts would have you believe, the point of an argument in a relationship is *not* to calmly smooth out the wrinkles that invariably come from spending long periods of time with someone. The point of an argument is to *win*.

Ergo,[14] the key to a long-lasting relationship must be to just keep the argument going until one of the sides calls a temporary truce. Or dies.

No end to the argument, no end to the relationship. See how easy that is? And I don't even *have* an advanced degree.

Psychologists have been wondering for years why men have the reputation for being aggressors and women have the reputation for being conciliators. Personally, I think they've missed the boat, or whatever it is psychologists do when they're wrong. Women

[14] From the Latin word *ergonomic*, meaning "I know more Latin than you, and I'm very comfortable with that."

are not conciliators. Women are able to keep relationships going because we have a secret. I've actually hesitated up to this point in the book to divulge this information, because this truly is the tool we have used since time began to keep our advantage in a relationship.

The secret is in knowing how to hold a really effective grudge. A well-crafted grudge, carefully placed in an argument, is an art form.

I don't think that anybody would dispute the fact that men have contributed many, many fine things to the arts. William Shakespeare, Leonardo da Vinci, "Weird Al" Yankovic . . . all truly masters of their domain. Yet holding a good grudge is an art form that men have yet to perfect.

This is because men operate under the delusion that what they are currently arguing about is the *actual topic of the argument.* Ha! Poor, misguided fools. To a woman, the topic of the current argument is anything that pops into her head. We have no official statute of limitations when it comes to dredging up various relationship infractions that happened in the past. And we have long memories.

Think of it as a mental chess game. The King may *believe* he's the most powerful piece in the game, but he is, in reality, severely limited in his ability to move around the board. The Queen, however, can move anywhere she wants, often through dimensions totally invisible to the King. For example, the King might *think* that the Queen is currently mad at him because he forgot to get her a gift for her birthday, but in reality the Queen is not only mad at that, she's also still thinking about the time he lied about switching places with the Rook just so he could be closer to the Knight, and is now *also* reminded of the time he told her he was going to be working late and she found out from the Pawns that he was really out drinking with the Bishop. So in the ensuing argument—and there *will* be an argument—the Queen once again brings up the Rook-switching incident, which, together with the Bishop-drinking thing and the forgotten birthday is proof positive that *you are having an affair,* **you lying, ungrateful bastard**! *After all I've done to protect you! Why would you lie to me like that?! Why?!*

Chess players will note that one of the rules of the game is that the match is not truly over until the King lies down and plays dead, which at that point is probably best for everyone involved.

My point here is that sometimes a relationship drifts into stormy waters, and dedicated partners have to take certain measures to right its course.

I used to work in advertising for a man named Erik, who had been transferred to our New York office from Denmark. Erik had a jagged scar where his right ear used to be and was married to the Danish Olympic sharpshooting silver medalist of 1984. These two points may not seem particularly relevant right now, but keep them in mind, because they figure into my story later.

Erik was the kind of guy who would regularly call us into his office for long, boring status meetings, and the only interesting thing that ever went on in those meetings was the jockeying we would do to sit on his earless side so that he wouldn't hear us talking about him. Just when you thought you would lapse into a coma from boredom, he would reach down and remove his shoes. Then he would remove his socks. From his desk drawer he would retrieve a pair of toenail clippers, and while some poor schmo was trying to focus on relaying his or her team's status, Erik would proceed to clip his toenails with relish. He was a jerk.

Now seems as good a time as any to add that he was also having an affair with his secretary.

One of Erik's favorite maxims, whenever someone was about to be fired or an account was on shaky ground, was, "Zümtimes ve yøøst haf to breck züm ecks to meck an ømelet." Since he was Danish, we were never really sure if that's what he *actually* said, but the logic is inescapable. If you really want that omelet—that long-term relationship— you *will* have to break some eggs.

Anyway, Erik's wife somehow found out about the affair (I like to think it was the Pawns who told her) and decided to pay a visit to her husband in his office. Erik was on the phone when she walked in and said something quietly to him in Danish. Pulling a small handgun calmly out of her purse, she fired once from across the office and shot the telephone right out of his hand, narrowly missing his one remaining ear. Turning silently on her heel, her head held high, she strode out of the office, her dignity intact.

From our hiding place in the supply closet, we all decided that it had to have been meant as a warning shot because the next thing we knew, Erik was definitely keeping his shoes on at the office, if you know what I mean. Shortly thereafter, he and his wife agreed that things would be even better for him if they moved back to Denmark. Erik's wife always could make one hell of an omelet.

Of course, not all of us are sharpshooters, and studies are inconclusive as to whether that really is an effective method for maintaining a long-term relationship anyway.[15] Most of us have to make do with an incredibly long memory and the ability to come up with creative ways to keep our advantage in

[15] The Publishers of this book, as well as our Legal Department, would like to take this opportunity to point out that they do not in **any way** endorse the use of firearms as a relationship tool, nor do they feel that it is an appropriate method for maintaining an open dialogue in *any* venue. We would also like to state for the record that the aforementioned story is largely made up, or so the author says, and that she put it in the book to be totally funny and snarky and make everyone laugh. Ha ha!

the relationship. Purely to keep it going long enough to propagate the species, of course. Certainly not because it's kind of fun.

Marnie is a divorced friend of mine who had been dating a guy named Brian for quite a while. If any couple ever supported my theory about perpetual arguing keeping a relationship alive, it was Marnie and Brian. We've all known couples like them. They could turn anything into a disagreement, and they would argue in public as well as in private. Their relationship thrived on the drama that was created, but they were totally committed to each other and united in their mutual quest to have the last word in their arguments. The relationship endured because every " . . . And that's *final*!" from Brian was inevitably followed up by an "Oh yeah?! Well, what about the time you . . . ?" from Marnie, and they'd be off again. It was a beautiful and moving example of Mother Nature's work at her finest, and it looked as if they were going to be together forever or until Brian won a fight, which everyone knows will never happen.

Eventually, their friends grew tired of listening to the bickering and suggested they follow the rules in one of the fair arguing books. Motivated by the thought of having no one to hang out with besides Marnie, and momentarily forgetting the importance of winning an argument at all costs, Brian came home one day with one of the books and suggested that the two of them sit down and follow the instructions for resolving their current feud, mostly so their friends would agree to have them in their homes again. Both of them took a seat opposite each other at Marnie's kitchen table, with the book between them.

"It says here," Brian began, "that we're supposed to start by agreeing to keep our voices down, and . . . "

"*You're* the yeller," Marnie pointed out. "I'm more of a pouter."

"Whatever. I won't yell if you don't yell. OK?"

"Fine. No yelling."

"We have to state what's bothering us in a calm manner," Brian continued. "It also says we should say it in the form of a factual statement like, 'Marnie, it upsets me when you make fun of my job . . . '"

"You sell joy buzzers and fake dog poo online."

"It's a website for serious collectors of fine novelty gags," Brian said, trying to remain calm. "Besides, you are supposed to wait patiently until I finish stating what's bothering me."

"It says that?" Marnie asked skeptically.

"Yup."

"And you're sure that this book isn't one of your gags?"

"NO! Stop trying to deep-six this. *No one will have us over anymore.*"

"I'm just saying that it sounds pretty abnormal, if you ask me," said Marnie, crossing her arms defensively. "And you're yelling."

"I'm sorry," Brian said, taking a deep breath. "Why don't you take a turn?"

"OK," Marnie said. "Brian, it really bothers me when you end every meal we eat with a Metallica song."

"I thought you liked heavy metal."

"Not when it's being burped at me."

"I didn't know that bothered you."

"You also leave the toilet seat up."

"But—"

"Oh, and novelty gags do NOT make good birthday presents for women."

"We're supposed to cover only one topic at a time!" Brian answered through gritted teeth. He was distinctly starting to feel outclassed, and his Fragile Male Ego could not take that. Feeling the balance of power shifting away from him, he blurted, "You know, I only started burping Metallica to distract myself from the fact that you have never *once* in our relationship attempted to pick up a check in a restaurant."

"Are you calling me cheap?!" Marnie exploded. This was a hot button topic, and Brian knew it.

Buttons are an interesting part of the whole argument/relationship dynamic. Everyone has buttons; they make us who we are. Some of us are sensitive about our looks, some of us feel secretly inadequate in the workplace. Some of us have so many buttons it's almost as if we were walking around totally highlighted, like a massive hyperlink. Buttons are a beautiful and necessary part of relationships, because they enable even the worst arguers to take advantage of another fundamental part of human nature:

IF A BUTTON EXISTS,
IT WILL BE PUSHED.

Seriously. Have you ever walked by a button and *not* pushed it just to see what would happen, or *not* clicked on a hyperlink online just to see where it would take you? Of course not. Or how about when you're waiting for an elevator: how many times have you seen someone walk up to the button, see that it's already lit, and then *push it anyway*? We're curious animals; we can't help ourselves.

Brian knew that Marnie had a reputation for being in possession of the first dollar she ever made, and that she was very sensitive about it. And since he was at a disadvantage in the relationship to begin with (remember the chess analogy?), he knew that the only way to regain his dignity would be to carefully select a button and push as hard as he could. Unfortunately for Brian, the particular button he selected might as well have been labeled "*Push Here to Find Out How You Are Going to Die.*"

"Are you for real?!" Marnie hissed. "Do you really want to go there?"

"Well . . . a-am I wrong?" Brian stuttered with feigned indignity, suddenly not entirely sure that he *did* want to go there.

"Let me tell you something. When I met you, you were a Hawaiian-shirt-wearing, *Battlestar Galactica*–watching geek with a whole lot more whoopee cushions and fake vomit than any grown man should have. All you could talk about was this stupid website you were planning to sell your toys on, and I had no way of knowing whether you could take me out in the style to which I am accustomed. So I let you pick up the first few meals to see what you were made of."

"They're *not* toys. They're collectibles. And how does that explain the coupon you gave me for my birthday?"

"That's not a coupon, it's a gift card for an hour-long massage!" Marnie said.

"But it says that *you're* the masseuse! Now *that's* ridiculously cheap," Brian shot back triumphantly.

They sat in silence for a moment, just staring at each other.

"OK, Brian," Marnie said softly. "What I think I hear you saying is that you feel disappointed by my lack of respect for your fair arguing technique and wish that I would be nicer about your job."

"Well . . . yes," Brian said, stunned by this sudden act of capitulation. Could he be heading for a win at last? "That's *exactly* how I feel."

"And you would like me to be more understanding about your intestinal eruptions, which I'm guessing also includes the farting in bed."

"Wait a minute. You promised you wouldn't keep bringing up my Irritable Bowel Syndrome. You know I can't help that . . . "

"You're right. That was unfair of me. I know how embarrassed you are about that. You know what? This might have been a good idea, after all. I think I have a much better understanding of where this is going now."

"You do?" Brian asked, mentally replaying the last few minutes of his life in a desperate attempt to see if *he* knew where this was going.

Marnie leaned forward seductively and placed her hand on top of his hand.

"Yes, I do. Why don't we celebrate this step forward in our relationship in the bedroom?"

"Well, sure . . . okay," Brian murmured softly, totally sucked in by his girlfriend's sudden and touching change of heart.

"Just give me a few minutes to get ready for you."

When Brian entered the bedroom, Marnie was lying in bed in his favorite nightgown and she had lit her most expensive scented candles, which flickered romantically in the darkened bedroom. She beckoned to him.

"Come to bed, Tiger," she purred.

As soon as he had removed his clothes and slipped into bed, he realized why Marnie had submitted so easily. The whoopee cushion he had given her for her birthday let out a sound that was not only startlingly realistic, but reverberated around the room with a humiliatingly long *"Pfthththfthththththtffftt thththththbththfthbthththhhhh . . . "*

Yup. To women, a good grudge is an art form.

And for you fair arguing experts out there, take it from us: It's not nice to fool Mother Nature.

CHAPTER 8

DIARY OF A RELATIONSHIP IN ONE FULL MENSTRUAL CYCLE

Christy's Journal: May 3

Spring's really here! Bought a whole new wardrobe to celebrate. Funny how those size 6 jeans used to fit so much better. Oh well, the snug look is in. Met a really cute guy named Mike at Le Bar last night. Amazing looking, and so nice! We talked for something like 45 minutes before he left. Said he had to get up early for work. It's such a relief to have finally met a normal guy. He took my number. Hope he'll text me. Have to get to the gym a little more; I can barely close my pants. I think I'll start walking to work.

Mike's "Friends and Family" Blog: posted May 12

Finally got started on that project at work. I can't believe how long it takes my asshole boss to make a decision. It's a good thing they only have one kind of toilet paper in the bathroom, or he'd be in there for the rest of his life. Found a wad of paper in my good Dockers last night. Looks like a phone number. Should I call it? Wish I could remember who the number belongs to. Hope she's at least decent looking. By the way, those Dockers are feeling a little tight around the middle; have to remember to pull off the button and use a safety pin from now on.

Christy's Journal: May 12

My friends said that if he doesn't text or call after a week, it's a no-go. Damn. He seemed interested. Plenty to keep me busy, though: just got a promotion at work, and I've been to the gym three times this week. Doesn't seem to be doing much. Oh well, these things take time. Cheated a little tonight by stopping off for a bag of those mini Hershey bars. Ate only one; decided that if I stay disciplined, I can have one mini bar of chocolate every day and it won't add too much to my total calorie intake. I am a paragon of restraint. I can't believe no one has ever thought of this before.

Mike's "Friends and Family" Blog: posted May 13

Called her. I was pretty toasted that night, but I vaguely remember meeting her now. Her name is Christy. Nice phone voice. Made plans to meet her back at Le Bar for drinks. Worked all weekend on the first phase of the project and my asshole boss didn't even notice. Putz.

Christy's Journal: May 15

He called! Ha! Why do I listen to my loser friends? Turns out he was just busy at work. It's so nice to meet a guy who is not a total slacker like my last boyfriend. We're going to meet for drinks tonight. What to wear??? I don't want to look like I'm trying too hard, but I don't want him to think I'm a slob either. At this point I would need a bucket of Vaseline and a giant shoehorn to get into my jeans. Definitely hitting the gym after work. My friends are coming over afterward to go through my closet and help me pick something out. Don't I have the best friends ever?

Mike's "Friends and Family" Blog: posted May 15

Got home and went for a run to cool off after the latest at work. Asshole boss is now trying to take credit for my work. I may have to kill him. Meeting Christy tonight. Found a shirt in my closet that passed the sniff test.

I'll just throw on a little extra cologne. Turns out I don't need the safety pin on my pants. I skipped lunch and now they fit just fine.

Christy's Journal: May 16

OMG, I think I'm in love! Mike is the nicest guy I've ever met. I'm not big on old-fashioned gallantry, but he *did* hold the door for me as we walked into the bar. I have to admit it felt nice. He wears a lot of cologne. Missed a deadline at work; how did I space out on that? Ate three Hershey minis this morning with breakfast; oh well, back on the horse tomorrow, right?

Mike's "Friends and Family" Blog: posted May 16

I like her. How many women actually reach for their wallet when the bill comes? Christy did. And she's pretty interesting; turns out she works in a business somewhat related to mine and she just got a promotion. I love a go-getter. We talked for hours and I walked her home. No jumping on this one. She has serious girlfriend potential. I don't even think she noticed the cologne. I'm going to call her for a dinner date first thing tomorrow.

Christy's Journal: May 17

Mike's a nice guy and all that, but it takes a lot of nerve to call someone in the morning and ask them out to dinner for that night. How does he know that I don't already have plans? Maybe he's just very confident in himself. Confidence is a good quality in a person, isn't it? If my last boyfriend had had more confidence, maybe he would have gotten up off the couch and gotten himself a job. Made it up to my boss for the missed deadline, and she was so pleased, she took me out for lunch. I had a salad and an unsweetened iced tea, and then we decided to be indulgent and ordered dessert. I ate mine and hers. She said she wasn't that hungry anyway. I guess I'll go out with Mike tonight but he's going to have to plan better in the future.

Mike's "Friends and Family" Blog: posted May 18

Boy, am I tired. Had a great time with Cindy last night. Whoops, sorry, that's my ex-girlfriend. Christy Christy Christy. Have to remember that. Better not call her in case I slip up.

Christy's Journal: May 18

How does a grown man *not* know to call a woman after a date? We had such a good time. I'm going to have to talk to him about that. Can't find the bag of mini Hershey bars. Must have finished them, but how is that possible?

Mike's "Friends and Family" Blog: posted May 23

At what point can you start calling someone your girlfriend? I guess Christy and I are "in a relationship" now, seeing as how we've seen each other every night this week. I can't stop thinking about her. She may be The One. I think I like everything about her. She even has that snarky sense of humor that I love in women. Last night she made this totally hilarious comment about how if we ever moved in together, there would be no room for her because of all of my *Battlestar Galactica* collectibles. We had a good laugh over that until I said, "Listen, in a Galactic Smackdown, my figurines wouldn't stand a chance against your collection of shoes." Somehow she didn't think that was quite as funny, but seriously, you can only walk in one pair at a time, right? How many shoes do you need? Having dinner with her again tonight. Have to remember to tone down the cologne and at least text her tomorrow.

Christy's Journal: May 24

Well praise be, he actually remembered to text me. And the cologne was much better, although I don't think he does his laundry regularly. Why haven't I noticed that he chews with his mouth open? Speaking of which, I chewed out my assistant at work today, although I can't remember what he actually did. Or did not do. But whatever it was—or wasn't—he'd better watch his step. Had a glass of chocolate milk with my Lean Cuisine lunch. How did I forget how good chocolate milk tastes? Must remember to pick up more Bosco.

Mike's "Friends and Family" Blog: posted May 24

Finished the project at work. Asshole boss actually stood up in the presentation and took credit for the whole thing. Haven't had anything to work on for a week. One of my buddies at work said people are starting to wonder whether I can "be part of the team" and why I'm so distracted lately. What the hell does *that* mean? And why are women so focused on the way they look, anyway? Christy asked me today if I think she's fat.

How do I answer that without getting myself into trouble? Googled the word "philtrum" on my BlackBerry when she wasn't looking. I didn't even know that part of the body *had* a name. Live and learn. I think she's mad at me just because I took her to Le Bar again for dinner. Something about how I always pick the restaurant or some crap like that. Half the time I don't even understand what she's talking about.

Christy's Journal: May 25
Screw the diet. Ate six Reese's Peanut Butter Cups today just on my lunch hour alone. I'm not talking to Mike right now because he's an ass, just like my last boyfriend. Why do I keep thinking that at least one of them will be different? If he loves Le Bar so much, let him eat there every night for all I care. But he's not going to be eating there with me, that's for damn sure. Bought an exercise DVD today called *Flat Abs Are for Closers: Tone Up the* Glengarry Glen Ross *Way."* The woman on the front of the box scares me a little, but I'm hoping it will help me lose some of the puffiness in the front. I think my assistant is avoiding me.

Mike's "Friends and Family" Blog: posted May 26

So I decided to be the bigger person and send her some flowers as an apology, although I'm still not sure what I'm apologizing for. You'd think she'd be happy, right? Wrong. She says that if you tape a bottle of Midol to the flowers, even as a joke, it doesn't count as an apology. What ever happened to her sense of humor? Asshole boss put me on notice today. He says I "lack focus." What a dweeb. I have plenty of focus. I mean, how does a person not appreciate a good Midol joke?

Christy's Journal: May 26

Is he kidding me? If that bastard thinks I'm going to accept his apology when he had the gall to attach a stinking bottle of *Midol* to a bunch of crummy daisies and then laugh about it, he really is deluded. He'd better be able to do a whole lot better than that. He doesn't know what he's up against. Wore the caftan to work today; nothing else fits. I wore it with my head held high, though, and I actually got a very sincere compliment from my assistant. It was hard to hear him from where he was perched inside the supply closet, but I'm pretty sure he said I looked nice. Maybe I can start a new fashion trend! The scary woman on the *Flat Abs* DVD says only losers eat chocolate, but what the hell does she know?

Mike's "Friends and Family" Blog: posted May 27

OK Christy, you want to make this personal? We'll make it personal. What kind of bitch sends a *Battlestar Galactica* DVD boxed set *and* a case of size XS condoms TO MY OFFICE? Keep the personal life personal, I say. Was moved from my office to a cubicle near the men's room. Asshole boss said it was because they hired some college kid intern with a fear of open spaces or something and he had to have four walls around him or he'd freak out. Bet I could show him a freak-out or two.

Christy's Journal: May 28

Oh. No. He. Didn't. Showed up for work today to find a box of extra-large tampons on my desk. How did I ever think this relationship was going to go anywhere? I actually thought this guy was nice! If I hear my assistant snicker one more time behind his computer monitor, I am *so* going to fire his ass. Returned the spring wardrobe. No sense keeping it when nothing fits. The Midol seems to be helping, I think.

Mike's "Friends and Family" Blog: posted May 29

Douche bags? Jeez, Christy, why don't you just say what you're *really* thinking? I never knew a woman could hurt me so much. At least she sent them to my apartment this time. I think I went too far with the tampons. She's really pissed at me. She won't pick up the phone, even though I tried calling her twice. Maybe three times. Took a few vacation days to deal with this. Asshole boss probably doesn't even know I'm gone. Damn, I'm tired. Haven't slept in two days. Can't eat. I really miss her. Better call a truce. I'll send her some of her favorite chocolates. I'm pretty sure she likes chocolate. Am I crazy or is my postman starting to look at me funny?

Christy's Journal: May 30

I can't believe he sent chocolate when he knows I'm trying to lose weight. What kind of sick, evil, twisted mind would do that? If he doesn't stop with the constant calling, I'm going to have to change my phone number. There are laws against stalking, or didn't you know that, Mike? I'm going to have to send him a firm, clear message once and for all. No point in stringing him along. Besides, men just aren't prepared to go toe-to-toe with women when it comes to symbolic relationship gestures. Speaking of symbolic gestures, my assistant quit today. Good riddance. Have gained 6 lbs. since the beginning of the month. A lot of good that gym membership is doing me. I've been going three times a week since the beginning of the month, sweating my brains out, and where has it gotten me? After dinner I finished the chocolates he sent and washed them down with some Bosco. Out of milk.

Mike's "Friends and Family" Blog: posted May 31

Stood outside her office building in the rain for what seemed like hours before she came out. God, I barely recognized her. When did she start wearing those tent dresses? Tried to ask her forgiveness and return the case of Preparation H she sent me for being, as she says, "a big asshole," but she wouldn't even talk to me. Can't take this anymore.[16]

Christy's Journal: June 3

Wow, *finally* got my period today and boy, I feel SO much better! Turns out it was all water weight. Not quite back into my jeans yet, but well on my way. Have to remember to get to the supermarket after work so I can return all of that Bosco. LOL, what was I thinking? Hired a new assistant. I think this one will fit in a lot better. Haven't heard from Mike for a few days; I wonder what he's up to . . .

[16] (Rest of entry accidentally deleted by author.)

FREQUENTLY ASKED QUESTIONS

Deb's Editor here. It has been brought to our attention that this book has actually raised more questions than it has answered, so in an attempt to ~~recoup our losses~~ tie together all of the loose ends, we have asked her to provide a helpful FAQ as a service to our readers.

1. I think that whole theory about Selective Deafness in Chapter 3 is total B.S. I play Call of Duty just like Anthony, and my girlfriend swears that I'm showing signs of . . . Dude, what're you doing?! Get DOWN!! Don't shoot at me, shoot at the @&%#ing enemy! IDIOT!!! Sorry, what was the question?

Asked and answered, Your Honor.

2. The other day my wife asked me if I thought the pants she was wearing made her look fat, and I told her no, that it's probably the family-size box of

Ring-Dings that she wouldn't share that was making her look fat. When she got mad, I reminded her, as the thoughtful husband I am, that her anger was probably due to the fact that she was very close to getting her period. Now she's not talking to me, and the Ring-Ding crumbs will not come out of my nasal passages no matter how much I blow my nose. What should I do?

Listen to me very carefully, because you do not have long for this world. You are in the advanced stages of Foot-in-Mouth Disease, and there's not much I can do for you anymore. The best you can hope for is to apologize. Then I want you to beg for her forgiveness and apologize again. Lather, rinse, and repeat as necessary. That way, when the end comes, you have at least a shred of hope that it will be swift and merciful. It was nice knowing you. Putz.

3. My boyfriend says that it's not fair when I bring up things from the past during our arguments, but how else can I convince him that he's wrong on just about every count? Evidence is evidence, right?

Of course it is. You and I know that, but men need help with this concept, and perhaps you're going a little too fast for him. Try to provide detailed audio-visual aids, as well as affidavits from friends and family members who have been witness to his multiple transgressions, whatever you imagine them to be. Men love that, and it's been shown in clinical studies that these sorts of personal attacks can actually help rewire a man's brain to bring his behavior more in line with what we expect from him. Then, when he's not sure whether he's coming or going, hit him with the Grudge From Hell. I've got $20 that says he'll stop whining about "fairness" after that.

4. How is Mike from Chapter 8 doing? I'm worried about him.

Mike is doing much better now, thanks. After he and Christy parted ways, and the XS condoms, the douche bags, and the Preparation H were all properly disposed of, Mike took an extended vacation at what he describes as a "gated community for the emotionally fragile" and now lives a peaceful existence on a Caribbean island running a restaurant he calls Le Philtrum.

A NOTE FROM THE AUTHOR'S FATHER

When my daughter Deb told me that she was leaving her high-paying corporate job (including major medical) to make her living as a writer, her mother and I were very proud of the fact that we didn't even flinch. "Go, be a writer," I believe were our exact words. So what if we sacrificed to send her to a very expensive private university for four years? Does it bother us in the slightest that she walked away from a respectable career in advertising—did I mention that this job had full benefits?—to sit, day after day, alone with that computer, banging out God knows what kind of drivel? As long as she's happy, we said to ourselves.

Then she starts with the crossword puzzles. This I could at least get behind, being a moderately talented solver myself, and who was prouder than me when she started getting her puzzles published in *The New York Times* by no less than Mr. Will Shortz himself? No one, that's who. And she's been in *The Washington Post*, and *The New York Sun*, and other places she tells me about when she calls to borrow money. Then, of course, she got involved making puzzles for those people at *The Onion* and landed herself that "X Games" column at *BUST Magazine* where they encourage all sorts of questionable stuff from her, although I don't even ask anymore. A father has his limits.

Now she writes a book on men and all of our faults, and all I can think is, *This is the thanks I get?*

As her parents, who love her no matter what her therapist says, her mother and I hope a lot of people buy this book. Maybe she'll stop calling us for money now, who knows? Incidentally, good luck finding it here in Florida, because my wife is making a new career for herself traveling to all of the bookstores in our area and buying up all the copies. She's not taking this nearly as personally as I am.

Of course, through all this, Deb *has* managed to stay married to the same very nice fellow for 20 years, which is not so easy these days, let me tell you. And she gave us two wonderful grandchildren.

So despite all of the agita she's caused us, she turned out pretty well, I think.

Her husband has the patience of a saint.

ACKNOWLEDGMENTS

This book would not exist without the much-appreciated contributions of the following people:

My wonderful editors at Sterling Publishing: Pamela Horn, for generously letting the genie out of the bottle, and Joelle Herr, for keeping me on track and for patiently responding to each and every one of the desperately insecure e-mails I sent her. You are both wise women and a joy to work with.

My incredible husband, David, an all-around great guy who taught me all about not giving up on my dreams and then made it possible with his love and support; Carly and Devin, the best kids any mother could ask for, who are unfailingly patient when I'm working and to their credit are not yet embarrassed by me (much); my beloved parents, Rose and Ira, for their love, encouragement and support and for being the first people to tell me I was funny in a good way; my wonderful sister, Sharon, and her family; and my awesome in-laws, Elinor, Seymour, and Jenny.

The Dunkin' Donuts Crew and all of my friends at home and abroad: You guys rock. Thank you for being truly happy for me that I got to write this book. Thanks also for helpfully offering to kick my butt if I got too uppity about it. That kind of emotional support is hard to find.

All of my friends, editors, and compatriots in the world of crossword puzzling: thank you for your support, friendship and inspiration. The amazing women of *BUST Magazine*, especially my editor, Emily Rems: Thanks for making me feel like a part of the family from the start and for being understanding about the deadlines. Editor Ben Tausig and my band of brothers at *The Onion/A.V. Club* Crossword Puzzle: Love you guys! Your collective talents set the bar unbelievably high.

Panera, for their bottomless iced tea, clean bathrooms, and free Wi-Fi.

And finally, a shout-out to Jade, my family's Extremely Spunky Border Terrier, for the kisses and long walks when I had writer's block, and who is a constant reminder that if you maintain the right attitude, practically anything can be considered food.

ABOUT THE AUTHOR

Photo by Nancy Shack

Deb Amlen is a humorist and crossword puzzle constructor whose work has been featured in the *New York Times*, *The Washington Post*, *McSweeney's*, *The New York Sun*, *The L.A. Times*, *The Chronicle of Higher Education*, and other respectable publications she tells her parents about when she calls to borrow money. She is also part of the outlaw posse that writes *The Onion/A.V Club* crossword puzzles and is also the "X Games" columnist for *BUST Magazine*—but don't bring that up if you run into her folks at the Early Bird Special. It just makes them crazy.

She lives in New Jersey.

Visit her on the web at www.debamlen.com.